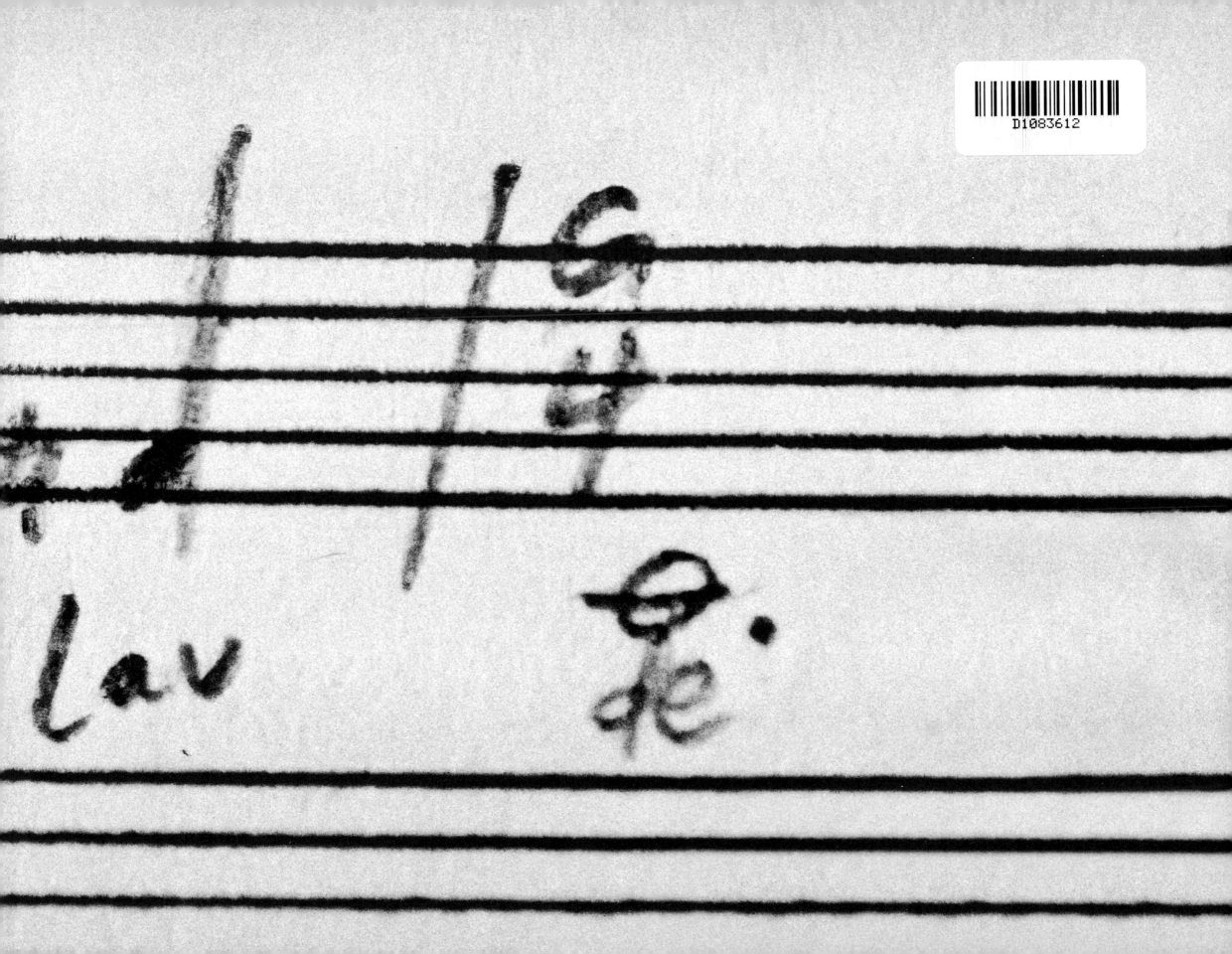

MAESTRO

Bradley Cooper

MAESTRO

ASSOULINE

INTRODUCTION

By Steven Spielberg

I was raised in a musical home. My mother was a concert pianist, my father was a music lover and Chopin, Debussy, Brahms and Mozart provided the soundtrack of my childhood. In 1957, my parents brought home the cast album from the original production of *West Side Story*. We played it over and over. Here was something very new: a musical tragedy told through a marriage of disparate harmonies and rhythms—classical, Tin Pan Alley, Puertorriqueño and Cubano—composed by a young artist whose career had already attained legendary proportions.

From virtually his first success as a conductor, Leonard Bernstein was omnipresent as a cultural figure, a titan of classical music, a revolutionary on Broadway, a pioneer in the use of television to educate and electrify the young. Watching him on CBS's *Omnibus,* my sisters and I were transfixed by Bernstein's charisma, his extraordinary erudition and his ability to convey to his audiences his marrow-deep passion for music, his thrilling ability to connect his chosen art form to other forms of human expression and to humanity itself. He made being an artist seem primal and glamorous, and he made the case that art was as essential to life as air and water.

And Leonard Bernstein was a Jew, of the generation of Jewish artists who refused to hide their Jewishness. Bernstein's mentor Serge Koussevitzky implored him to call himself Leonard Burns, warning him that no American orchestra would hire a conductor with a Jewish-sounding name. Bernstein responded, "I have decided to make it as Leonard Bernstein or not at all." The emergence, in the 1950s, of proudly Jewish public figures like Bernstein transformed more than the arts in America; they helped steer our country into a confrontation with and open conversation about anti-Semitism, part of a growing awareness of racism, discrimination and brutal oppression as threats to American democracy. With his score for Jerome Robbins's ballet *Dybbuk*, with his Jeremiah Symphony, in his long association with the Israel Philharmonic, with his devotion to the music of Gustav Mahler, Bernstein's Jewishness was central to his art and to his public persona. Successive generations of Jewish artists, including me, are deeply in his debt.

I've always imagined that being the conductor of an orchestra must resemble, at least in some ways, being a film director. Each takes printed material, a script or a score, brings it into a community, a complex collaboration with a host of highly skilled artists, technicians, producers. Then tries her or his or their best to inspire, negotiate, cajole, argue, wave their arms around, hide their private fears and share confidence and excitement, all in the hope that, out of a collective effort always threatening to collapse into chaos, something powerful, profound, delightful, challenging and/or entertaining, something of real meaning and value for an audience, will emerge.

Partly due to my imagined affinity with orchestral conducting, as well as to my fifty-years-long love affair with his music, I began several years ago to consider making a film about Leonard Bernstein. I realize now that, among other factors, one of the catalysts for me in my decision to try to make the film was that I felt I'd found an actor who seemed to me perfect to play Bernstein: Bradley Cooper. At one of our first meetings, before I'd mentioned the idea of the film, Bradley

told me that when he was a kid he'd dreamed of becoming a conductor, and even better, he'd spent hours listening to Bernstein recordings, conducting an imaginary orchestra. I couldn't believe my ears. I said something like "Funny you should mention that…"

At the time, Bradley was in post-production for *A Star Is Born,* his directorial debut. I loved the film. I was especially thrilled by the masterful way in which Bradley, as co-writer and director, had woven together the story's drama and music—even more impressive that he'd achieved this while turning in a searing performance. More than a triple-threat stunt, Bradley's deep involvement in his film, writing, directing and acting, felt necessary somehow to his discovery of new fire in *A Star Is Born*'s often-told tale. It seemed clear that, in addition to playing the lead character, Bradley had to take the helm. Our film about the Maestro had found its intended director.

Casting off the expectations and conventions that accompany biographical films, Bradley and co-writer Josh Singer found an innovative way to explore this legend's life and to reveal the love story at its core, Bernstein's tortured and enduring love affair and marriage to Felicia Montealegre—as portrayed with overwhelming, incandescent grace by Carey Mulligan. Bradley's portrait of Bernstein merges artist and subject to an extent that's nothing short of uncanny. And the film, ultimately, is his vision of artistic, sexual and romantic obsession, of great love and great loss, of familial bonds and terrifying loneliness. When Bradley Cooper raises his baton, we are in the hands of a *MAESTRO*.

The pilot light I needed to make *Maestro* turned on many years ago, when I was in grad school—before I actually came across the project. When I decided I would direct the film, I went into a deep dive of research on Lenny and his family and just immersed myself in learning as much as I could about every aspect of this life. Once I let everything soak in, I realized the most interesting and relatable aspect to me was this marriage between Lenny and Felicia. It was an unorthodox, genuine love that I found endlessly intriguing. This is the story I wanted to tell, a love story. Of course, the other irreplaceable element was the music, the great works both composed and conducted by Bernstein that serve as the score within the film. I've listened to this music for so long, going back to when I was a child. This journey has taken six years, and I will be forever grateful to Jamie, Nina and Alex Bernstein for letting me into their family and their hearts and who continue to walk alongside me throughout all of this. It has been one of the greatest joys of my career to bring this story to life.

Bradley Cooper

Concept art by Alexios Chrysikos.

Above: First production meeting.

"A work of art does not answer
questions: it provokes them; and its
essential meaning is in the tension
between the contradictory answers."

LEONARD BERNSTEIN

Quote from "Bernstein: What I Thought...," published in *The New York Times,*
October 24, 1965, and later collected in Bernstein's book *Findings.*

"One thing is for sure, I have never made art as fearlessly. His story forced me to be fearless, because he was. That was the biggest gift that Lenny gave me."

BRADLEY COOPER

"*Maestro* is born of a mind palpably in love with the movies, and that energy is contagious. It's a Leonard Bernstein fever dream. The film puts to use techniques originally used in musicals of Hollywood's Golden Age, married to the depth and realism of its human portraits to offer a totally modern statement. The performances are patient and measured— in a word, breathtaking. The final result is an ode to a past world treated with maturity and grace. I have never seen another movie like it."

RICK RUBIN

Opposite: (*left*) Felicia Montealegre Bernstein and Leonard Bernstein, 1953. Photographed by Erio Piccagliani.

"I hope after audiences have seen the film they feel like they were taken away into a world that will resonate with them. A world of people, of emotion, of a time period, that they went on a trip and that it stays with them. I hope they see the humanity in the story. I certainly do."

KEVIN THOMPSON, *production designer*

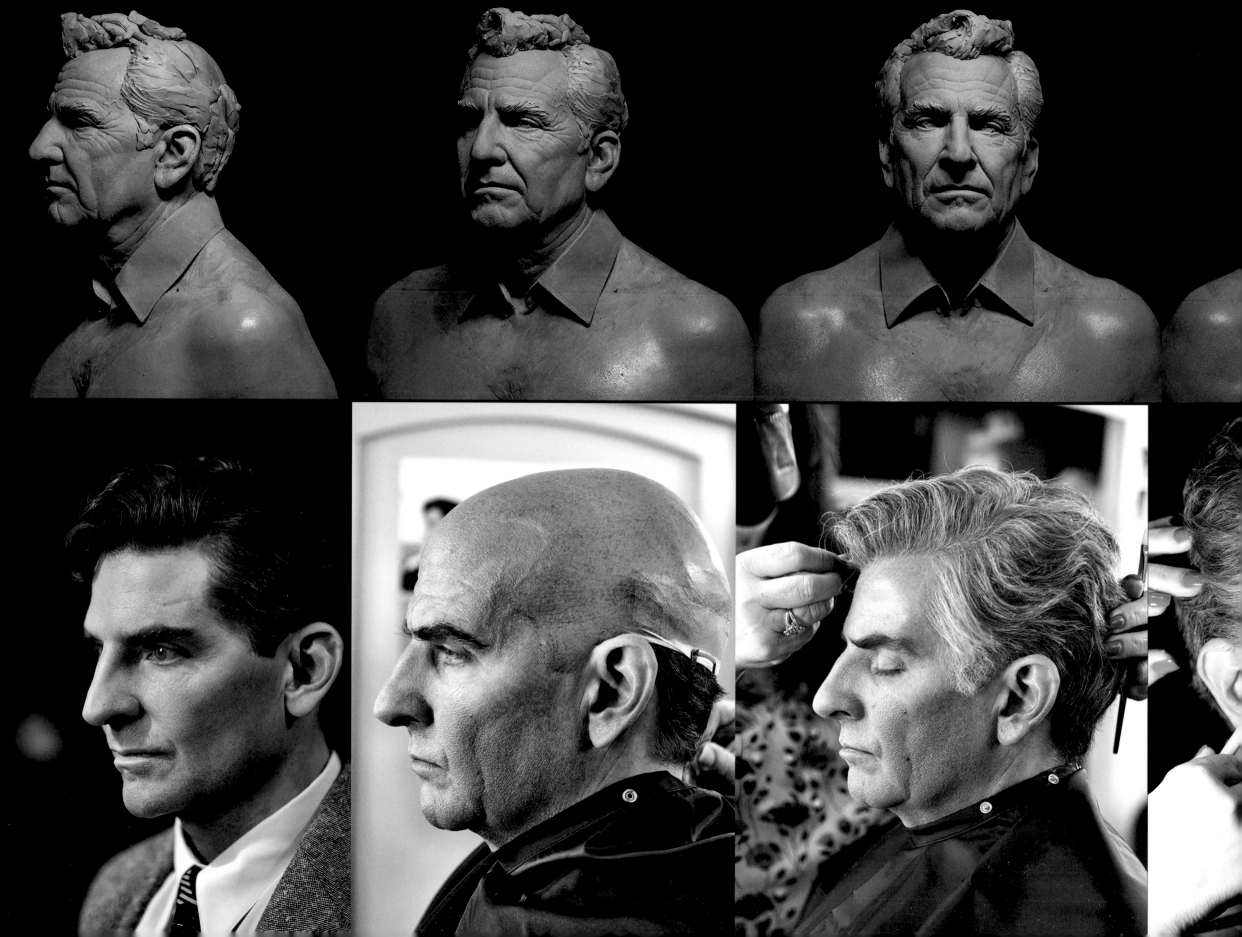

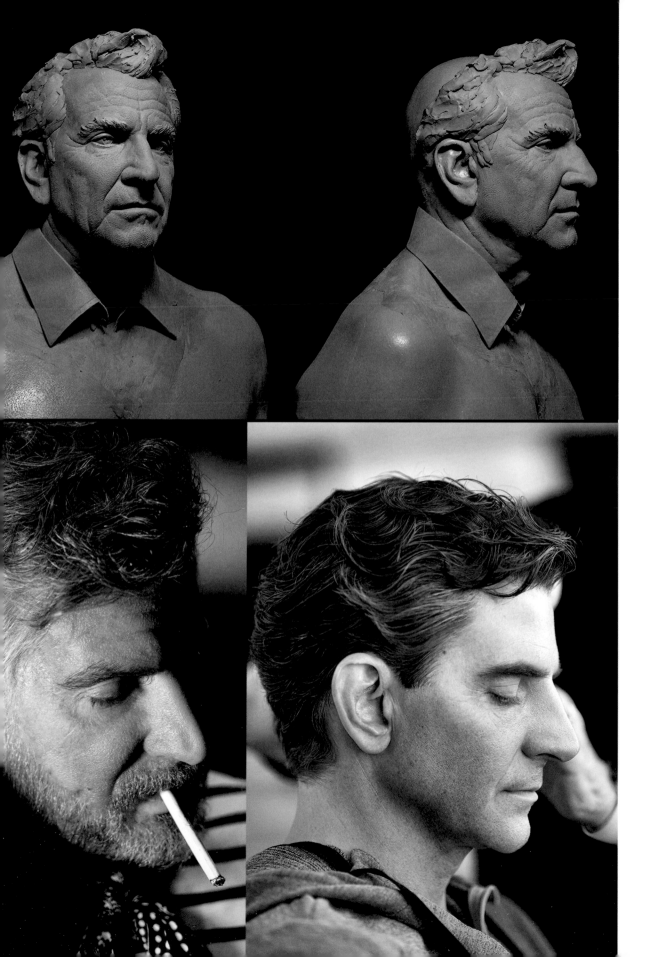

"So Bradley is not too far from Lenny, but we wanted to put the essence of Lenny on Bradley's face. And whenever I try to design the likeness on an actor's face, I want to respect both the original person and the actor. And they have to merge together in a good balance."

KAZU HIRO, *prosthetic makeup designer*

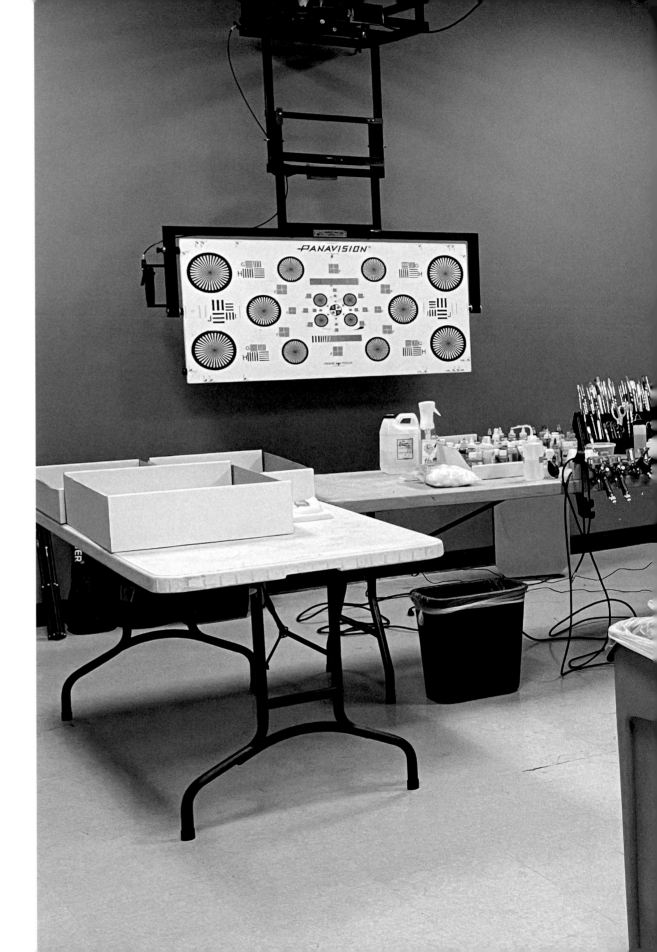

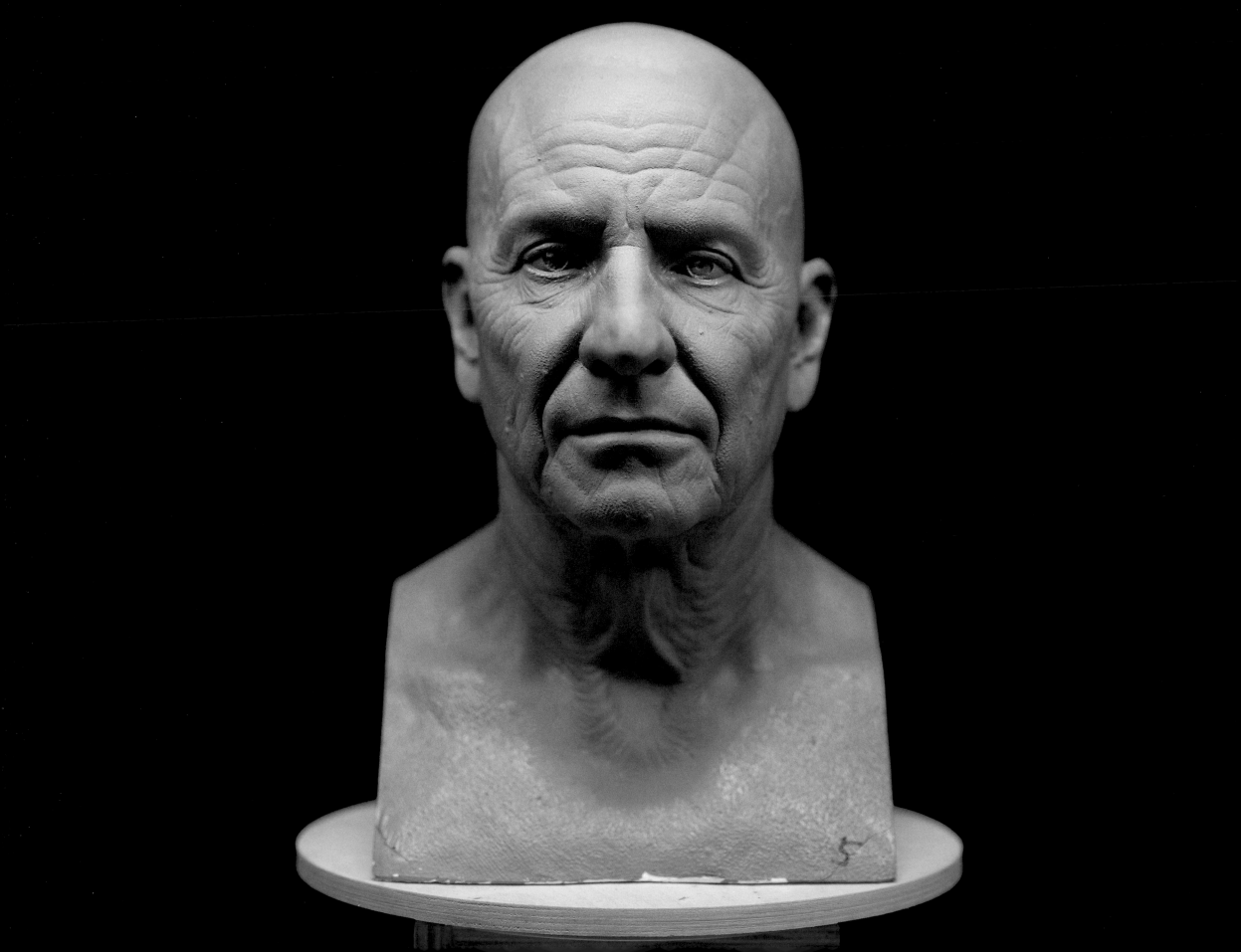

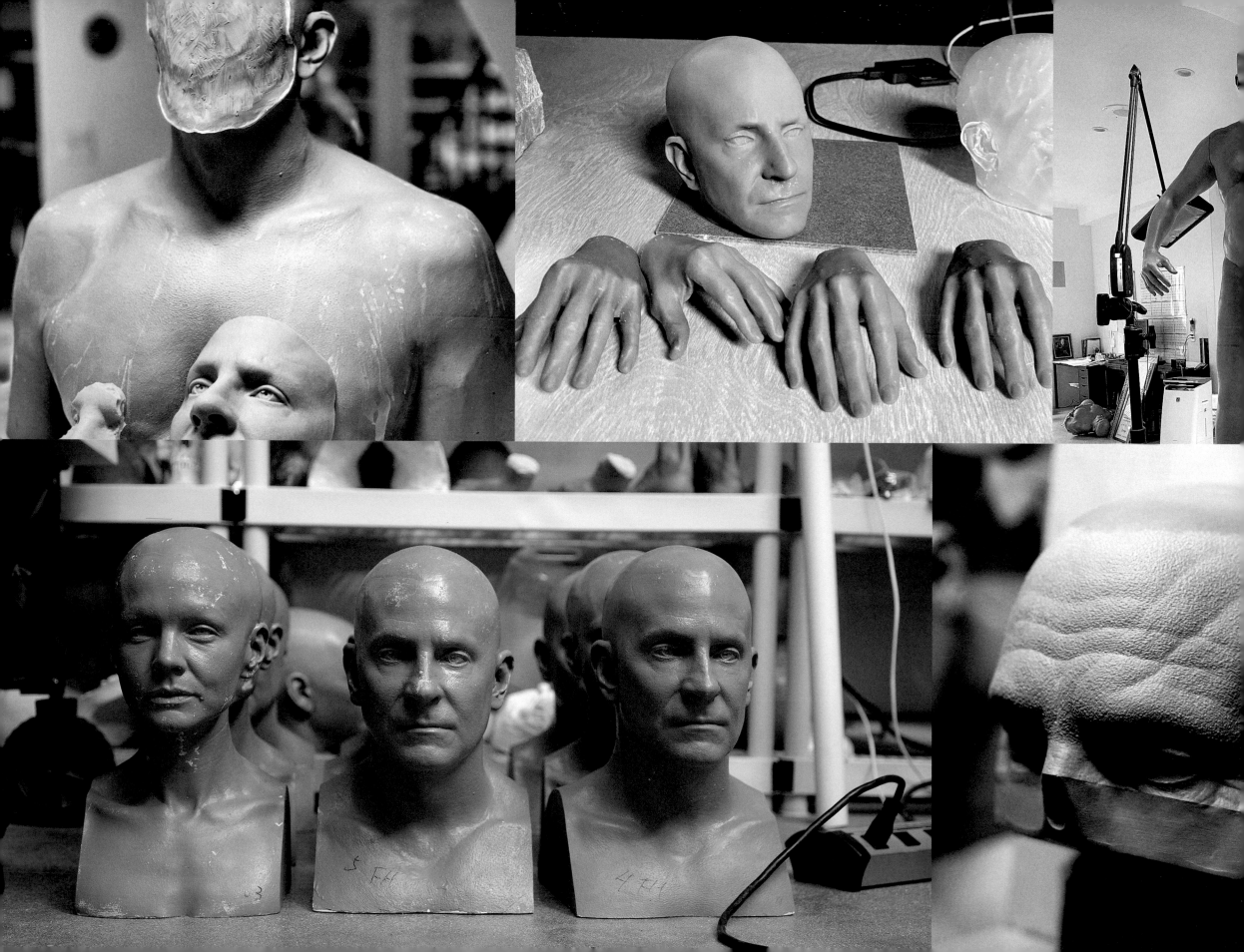

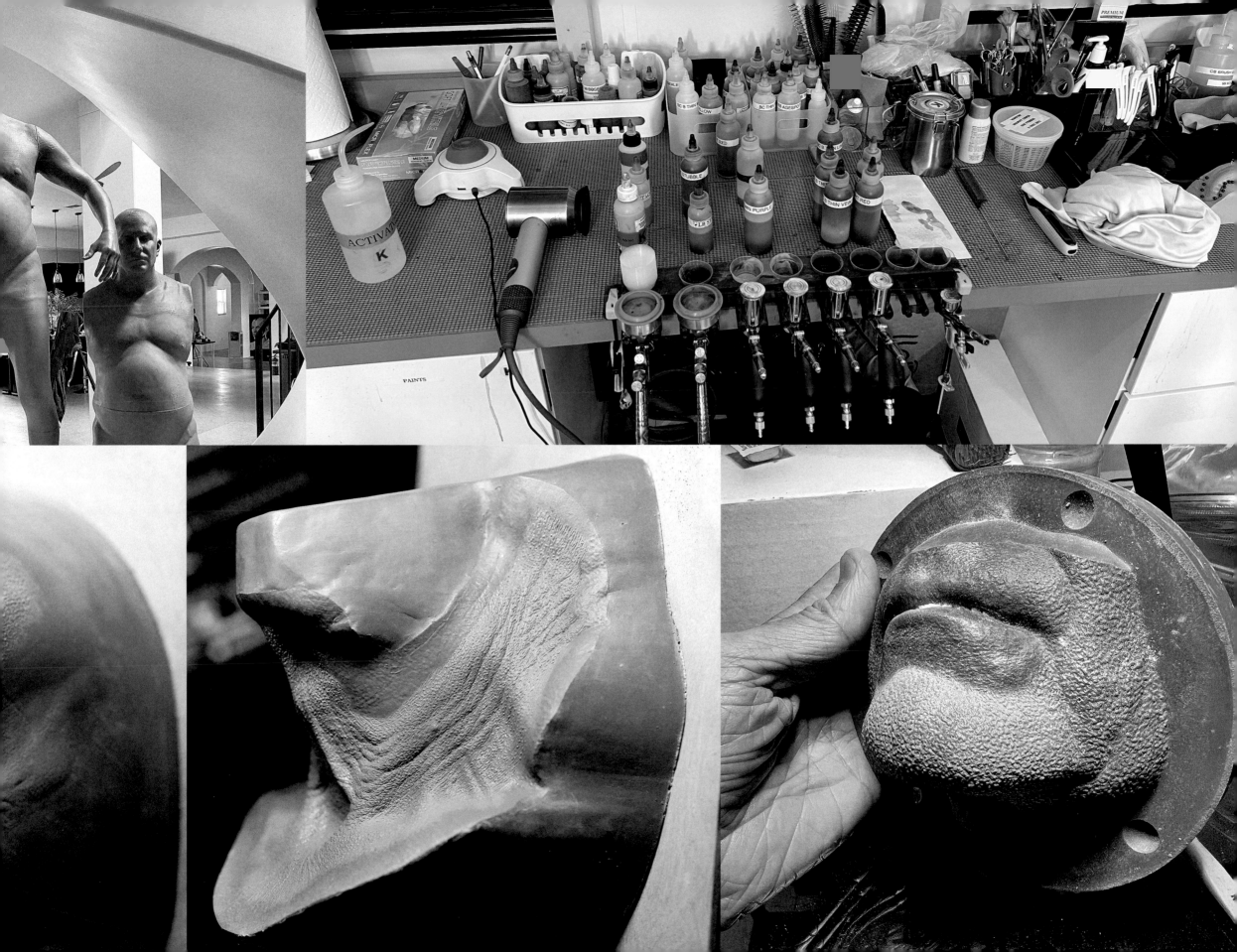

"The prospect of going from 1943 to 1989 was fantastic. Thrilling, and a bit daunting. The question is always 'How am I going to tell this story?'"

MARK BRIDGES, *costume designer*

CARDIGAN JACKET.
    SERJ

PANTS- PIORT

Tshirt

SHIRT.

BELT

SHIRT AND
    TIE   Long tie.
JACKET serj
    Repeat
    Stranghe

LB prop watch

Scene: 20, : (2) LEONARD BERNSTEIN, **Change**: 7   **Scene**: 20, : (2) LEON

24 FPS   FOOTAGE: 391

Scene: 21, : (2) LEONARD BERNSTEIN, **Change**: 7   **Scene**: 22, : (2) LEON

24 FPS   FOOTAGE: 68

Scene: 22, : (2) LEONARD BERNSTEIN, **Change**: 7   **Scene**: 22, : (2) LEON

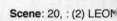

LB
TANGLEWOOD 1946

MAESTRO
Directed by Bradley Cooper
COSTUME DESIGN
Mark Bridges

LB
Connecticut 1971

MAESTRO
Directed by Bradley Cooper
COSTUME DESIGN
Mark Bridges

FELICIA
Arrau Party 1946

MAESTRO
Directed by Bradley Cooper
COSTUME DESIGN
Mark Bridges

Scene: 12, : (1) FELICIA, **Change**: 2

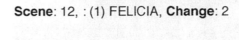

Scene: 12, : (1) FELICIA, **Change**: 2

Scene: 13, : (1) FELICIA, **Change**: 2

Scene: 13, : (1) FELICIA, **Change**: 2

LB
Tanglewood party 1989

MAESTRO
Directed by Bradley Cooper
COSTUME DESIGN
Mark Bridges

FELICIA
Kennedy Center
MASS Premiere 1971

MAESTRO
Directed by Bradley Cooper
COSTUME DESIGN
Mark Bridges

LB
Thanksgiving 1971

MAESTRO
Directed by Bradley Cooper
COSTUME DESIGN
 Mark Bridges

"One of the interesting things about Felicia was how much she changed her hair. Every couple of years, she changed the style, the color, you name it. We decided to simplify that, to narrow down her looks. It made more sense to change it when there was a time jump in the storyline."

KAY GEORGIOU, *hair department head*

FELICIA
Ely Cathedral 1976

MAESTRO
Directed by Bradley Cooper
COSTUME DESIGN
Mark Bridges

FELICIA
East Hampton House
Friends visit 1978

MAESTRO
Directed by Bradley Cooper
COSTUME DESIGN
Mark Bridges

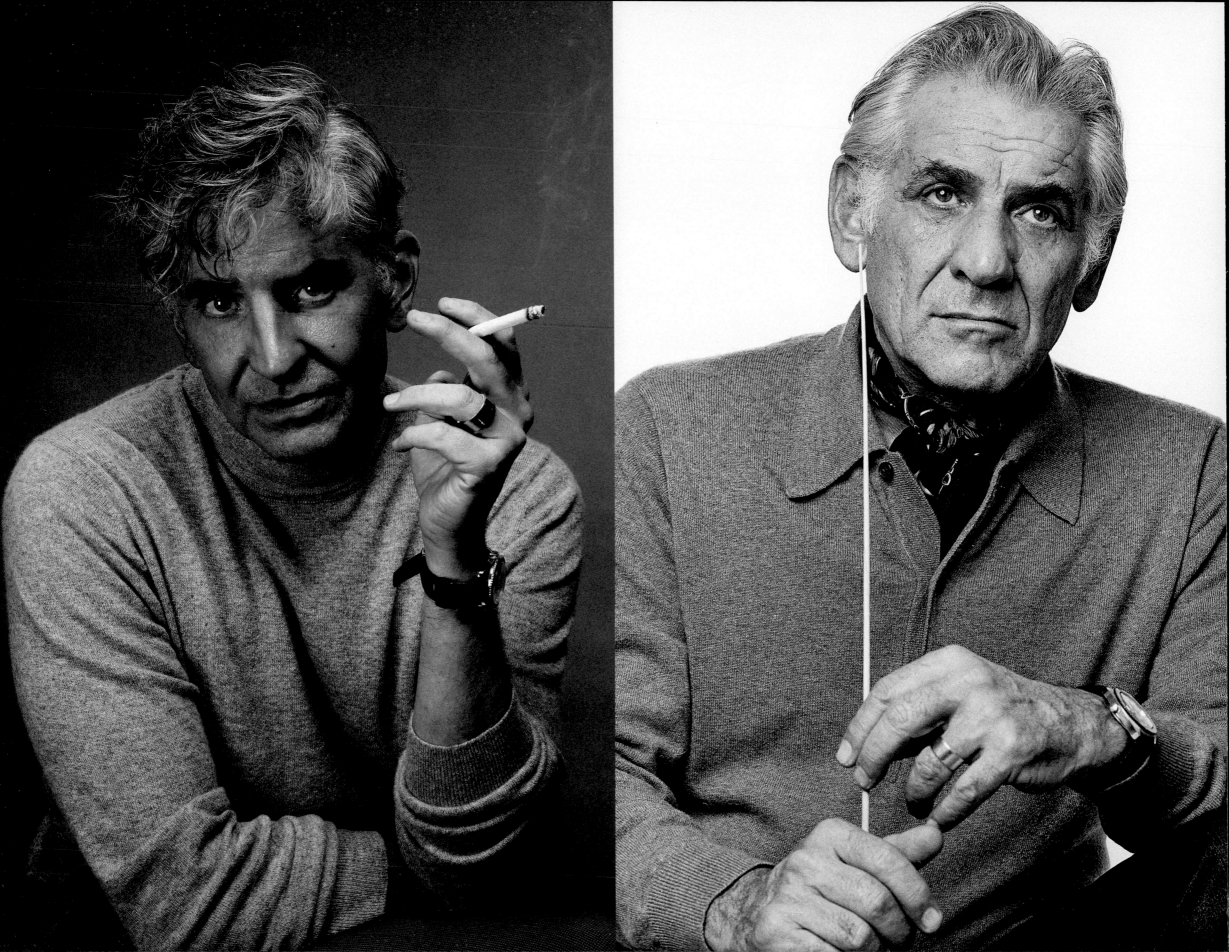

"In *A Star Is Born,* the nuclear weapon was always Lady Gaga's voice. For *Maestro* I figured it was mine to mess up because I had a nuclear weapon and that's Leonard Bernstein's music. Just the breadth of it, how diverse it is and how moving it is."

BRADLEY COOPER

Opposite: (*right*) Leonard Bernstein, 1978. Photographed by Jack Mitchell.

"Felicia was just such a massive job. It was just the most exciting part and felt akin to some of the roles that I've been privileged to play onstage but had not found the equivalent of on-screen so much. It was so rich, and there was so much breadth to her character and so much change in her life. I was just amazed that [Bradley] was asking me to do it."

CAREY MULLIGAN

"[Bradley] really got Bernstein. It was insane, every gesture, every facial expression. What I needed to do was to guide him with how it relates exactly with the orchestra in real time."

YANNICK NÉZET-SÉGUIN, *conductor*

MY MAESTROS

By Jamie Bernstein

There was no reason for my brother, my sister and me to assume that Bradley Cooper would wind up striving for authenticity to the degree that he did. This was a work of art, after all: a creation, *his* creation. Once we'd given him the go-ahead to make this film about our father, we knew we had willingly turned the reins over to him. It was his project, his film. And we were okay with that.

What we did not expect was that Bradley would go to such extraordinary lengths to include us in his long, deep process of discovery. He texted, he visited, he asked questions and then he asked more questions.

And he sent lots of photos. We gaped into our phones as the extraordinary makeup artist Kazu Hiro went through his alchemical process of turning Bradley into Lenny. Sometimes, in certain shots, at certain angles, the resemblance was so shockingly accurate that it would make us gasp.

We were particularly disarmed by Bradley's evocation of our father's joy around us kids. Leonard Bernstein was not what you would call a hands-on parent—he didn't cook dinner or attend too many of our school assemblies—but his delight in our company was always there. We felt treasured. Bradley found so many ways to convey this sensibility: from receiving Jamie's drawing as it fluttered down the stairwell, to cuddling baby Alexander on the tree swing, to clutching teenage Nina at a moment of unbearable crisis.

Photos of Leonard and Felicia Bernstein with their three children: Jamie, Alexander and Nina.

And then there was Carey. She zoomed with us from England several times, asking us countless, fascinating questions about our mother, Felicia. She even went all the way down to Chile, to get a sense of the environment where Felicia had grown up, and to meet our mother's ninety-eight-year-old brother-in-law.

Felicia Montealegre was a unique creature: nuanced, tricky to explain, let alone capture in a performance. Even as we described her to Carey, we struggled to capture her subtleties. So we were beyond astonished to see what Carey was able to achieve in the film. While Bradley strove to physically resemble our father at various stages of his life, Carey was not trying to look exactly like our mother—and yet somehow she was able to evoke Felicia's essence. We may never get over it. (We may also not get over having to watch our mother die, again and again.)

In my memoir, *Famous Father Girl,* which came out in 2018 (Bernstein's centennial year), I described one of my last conversations with my mother in the days before we lost her. She said to me, "Always remember: *kindness*. Kindness, kindness, kindness." Her oracular words have never left me. As part of his copious research, Bradley had read my book. Incredibly, this very moment I described wound up in the film. Carey's performance in this scene is, for me, devastating.

Throughout his long process of inquiry, writing, pre-production, shooting and then several iterations leading to the final cut, Bradley included us three sibs in all of it: seeking out our reactions, searching for the words to explain his process, even weeping with us sometimes. The degree and quality of his involvement went far beyond anything we could have imagined.

It's all quite disorienting. Bradley is younger than we are, yet he's playing our dad—and playing him at different ages, meaning that "we" appear at different ages in the film, too. All this immersion in our family past leaves us feeling like we don't quite know what year it is or how old we are. Are we little kids, are we teenagers, are we grown-ups with kids of our own? Is our dad younger or older than we are now? These questions become especially keen as we watch the scenes shot at our own family place in Connecticut. It's like having your life twirled inside a kaleidoscope.

All of which is why, when friends and relatives ask, "What do you think of the film?," we have to explain that we are the three least equipped viewers on the planet to be objective. Okay, we're pretty sure it's an extraordinary work…but we're 100 percent certain that Bradley put every ounce of himself into this film, and successfully conjured up the mysterious, magical vibe of our family: Lenny and Felicia's family. How the hell did he do that?!

LB

So I had no choice but to
become the composite of adopted
speech, manner, and outlook on life,
a composite which enables me to be
many things at once -- and that's
why we, you and I, are able to
endure and survive. Because the
world wants us to be only one thing,
and I find that deplorable.

FELICIA
There are many things stopping me, Lenny, but fear
isn't one of them. I wouldn't be standing here in
front of you, heavens, I wouldn't even be in New York
City if fear had gotten the better of me. It's just
not that easy. We'd be fools not to think that luck
plays a part as well as talent and determination.

FELICIA
And don't forget you are
a man.

LB
I never do.

They look into each other's eyes. She places a
hand upon his cheek.

FELICIA
(a whisper)
Those eyes... You don't even know
how much you need me, do you?

LB
(whispers back)
I might.

MURROW
Lenny, what's the big difference in
the life of composer Bernstein and
conductor Bernstein?

Felicia's heard this answer before, but she
forces a smile.

LB
Well, I suppose it's a difference --
it's a personality difference which
occurs between any creator versus
any performer. Any performer,
whether it's Toscanini or Tallulah
Bankhead or whoever it is, leads a
kind of public life. An extrovert
life, if you will; it's an
oversimplified word but something
like that. Whereas a creative person
sits alone in this gray studio that
you see here and just writes all by
himself and communicates with the
world in a very private way and
lives a rather grand inner life
rather than a grand outer life.
(then)
And if you carry around both
personalities, well, I suppose that
means you become a schizophrenic and
that's the end of it.

LB laughs at his own joke,
glancing at Felicia, who smiles;
it's genuine, her delight in him.

FELICIA
If summer doesn't sing in you, then
nothing sings in you. And if nothing
sings in you, then you can't make music.

The MUSIC CONTINUES as LB and David walk.
Neither of them says a word.

And after some time, LB stops. This is where it
ends. David turns to him.

David extends his left hand and caresses LB's
cheek. LB takes in that moment of intimacy
while simultaneously glancing across Central
Park South at some people looking at him.

LB
You see those people across the
avenue? Staring at us...?

He does.

LB (CONT'D)
Saying, "It can't be him, he's much
better-looking on television, isn't
he? Certainly has Leonard
Bernstein's ears, doesn't he?"

They laugh together.

LB (CONT'D)
"Can that be him? Is it possible?"

LB, still half-glancing across the street, has
nothing more to say.

HARRY
I guess denial is not just a river in Egypt.

LB
That was the crossword last week,
three letters. Do you know what it is?

TOMMY (O.C.)
Pun.

LB turns and finds TOMMY COTHRAN, twenty-five.

LB
(delighted)
Yes, it is pun.

TOMMY
Yes, it is.

LB
Did you do the Thursday?

TOMMY
Yes, I did.

LB
It's quite easy but --

TOMMY
That was row five.

It catches LB. He resets.

LB
I have one or two saving
factors, John. One is that I love
people. And I love music. I love
music so much it keeps me glued to
life even when I'm most depressed.
And I can get very deeply depressed.
But I have a work ethic, and that
keeps me afloat. And the other is
that I do, I love people so much
that it's hard for me to be alone.
Which is part of my struggle as a
composer.

GRUEN
Yes, you're the only person I've
ever met who leaves the bathroom
door open for fear of being alone.

LB
I mean, can one really believe that
man is just this trapped animal who
is a victim of his own greeds and
follies? Either one believes in the
divine element in this or one
doesn't. And as long as I believe
it, which I assume is why I love
people so much, then I have to
believe that in some remote corner
of my soul there is a way out.

EXT. BACKYARD, FAIRFIELD – CONTINUOUS

The MUSIC CONTINUES as Felicia, fully
clothed, jumps in the pool. We GO WITH HER,
underwater... the bubbles surrounding her as
she sinks. Felicia stays motionless in that
moment, a sense of peace perhaps in the escape
of it all, maybe not wanting to come back up,
maybe preferring to stay, as if she could stay
here frozen in amber.

FELICIA
No, let's not make excuses... He
didn't fail me.

SHIRLEY
Felicia...

FELICIA
No, it's my own arrogance...to
think I could survive on what he
could give... It's just so ironic, I
would look at everyone, even my own
children, with such pity because of
their longing for his attention.

It was sort of a banner I wore so
proudly, "I don't need, I don't
need." And look at me now... Who's
the one who hasn't been honest? I
miss him, that child of mine.

They both just look at each other.

FELICIA
Any questions?

FELICIA
There's no hate. There's no hate.
There's no hate in your heart.

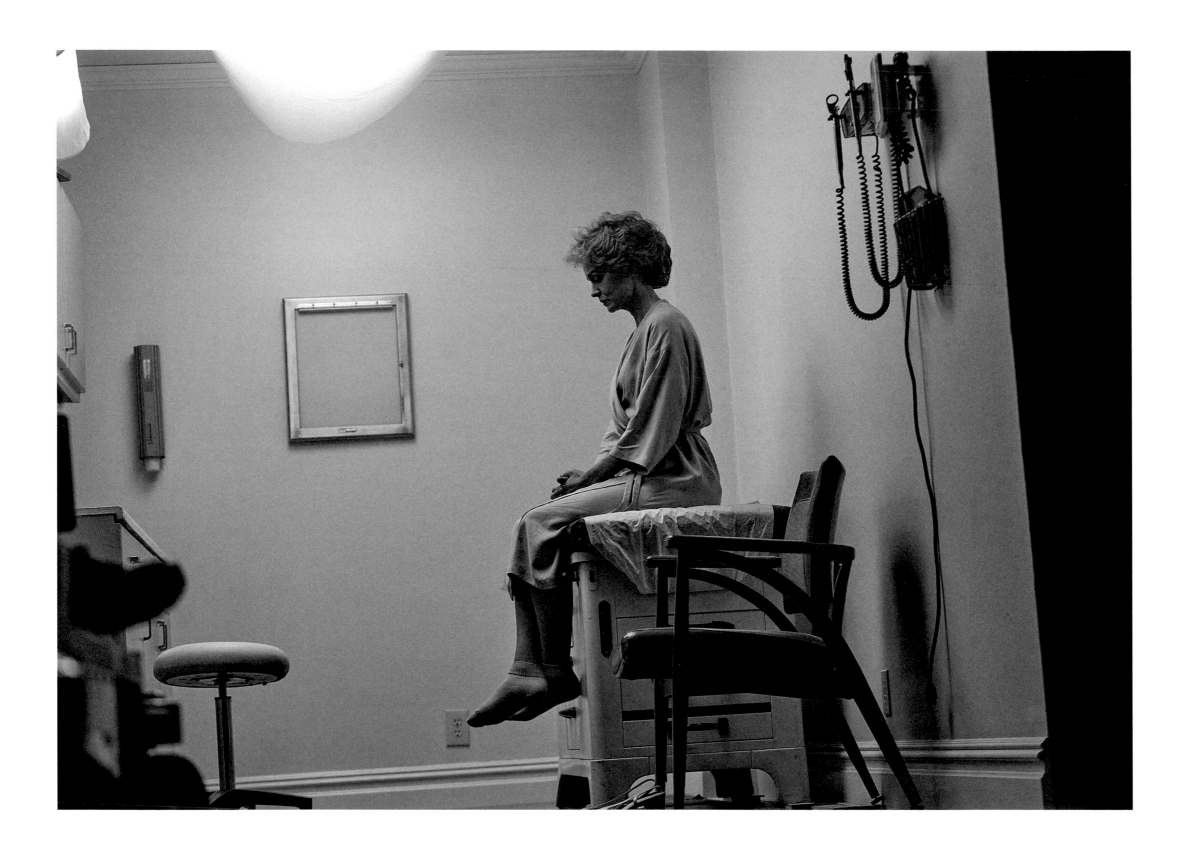

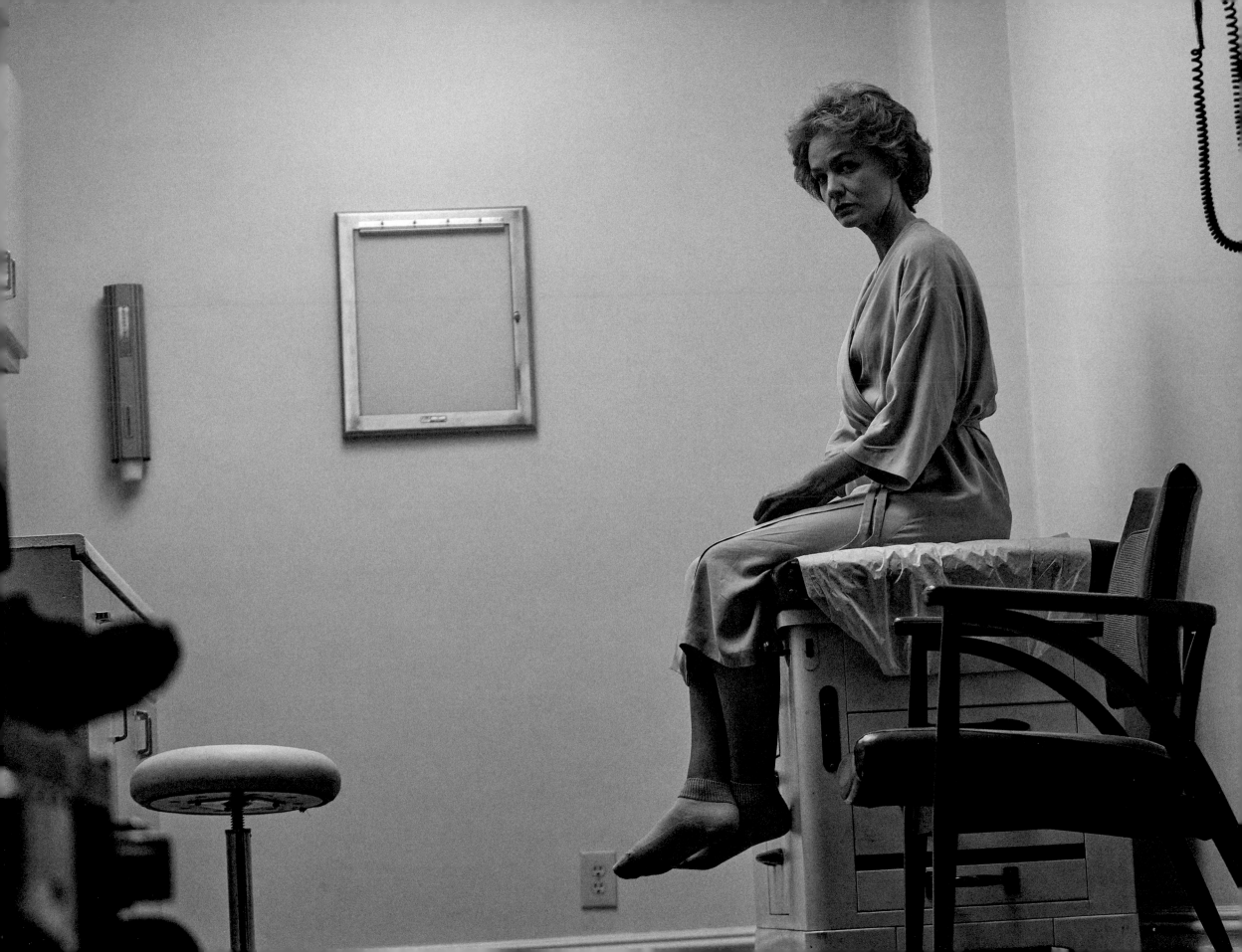

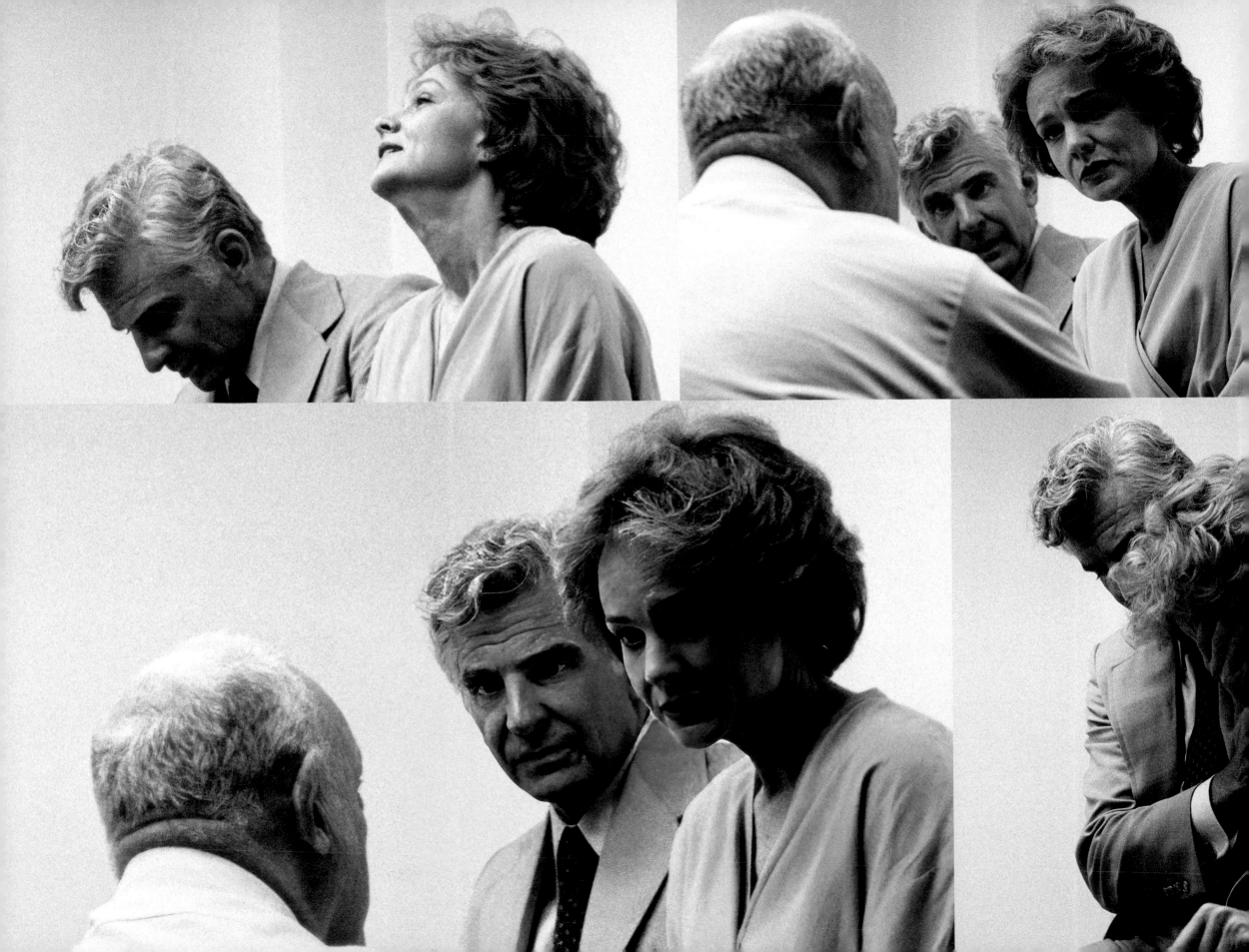

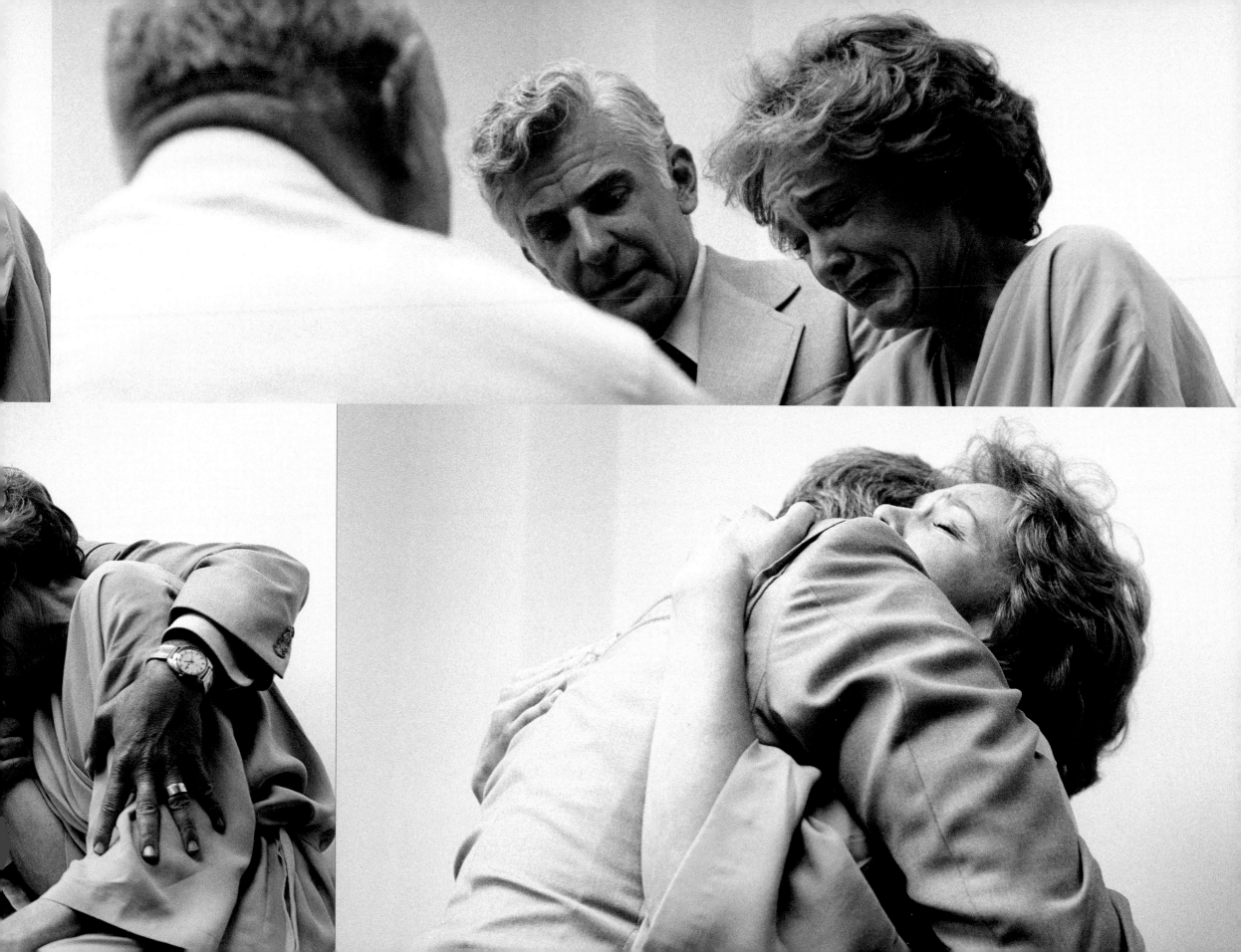

She puts on the Shirley Ellis single, and we hear the cymbals that mark the beginning of "The Clapping Song." We go WIDE on a sprawling house. A beautiful, summer day. As the music kicks in, the three grown children start to dance. Jamie, Alexander, with Nina jumping in. And when it gets to the chorus they all point to Felicia and sing...

JAMIE/ALEXANDER/NINA
My mother told me if I was goody,
that she would buy me a rubber dolly.

LB smiles as he gets up, turning to Felicia and taking her hand. She resists, but LB pulls her up with him into a gentle dance.

LB
(to the kids)
Come here, everybody.

The family comes in for a group hug, enveloping Felicia with love, "The Clapping Song" playing all the while.

FELICIA

All you need, all anyone needs,
is to be sensitive to others.
Kindness. Kindness. Kindness.

LB
Something she told me when I was
gloomy about something, and I
decided to say an Edna St. Vincent
Millay poem, which then became
Songfest. But summer does still sing
in me. Not as strongly as it used to
or as often. But it sure does. If
not, I would have jumped into the
lake long ago.

LB takes a long drag, contemplative. Then

LB (CONT'D)
Any questions?

ANATOMY OF A SCENE

Dakota Fight

It's hard to pinpoint the origin for the composition and execution of a scene. For the fight scene at the Dakota, I would probably have to connect it back to when I was a child observing my parents argue, from a distance at the top of the stairs. Positioning the lens in between Lenny and Felicia fighting was never an option—that's safe. As a viewer, I would become aware that I'm watching a movie. But put me at a distance—peering in—and all of a sudden there is tension and it's real and I'm no longer safe. The tension could then pour over onto me. So that, in part, dictated the lens and position. Throughout the film, the camera is at various distances from Lenny and Felicia, to, hopefully, evoke an emotional reaction from the audience: longing to belong, fearing things are not what they once were, being intoxicated by the love and romance and whimsy, wanting to avoid what's happening, feeling unworthy of belonging or being struck by the realism of life.

I also wanted the punch line of the joke to hit. And the joke can work only if we stay in this shot until Snoopy appears outside during the Thanksgiving Day Parade. If we cut back to a wide view so that Snoopy can appear, it becomes premeditated and self-conscious, and as a viewer I would be aware of the cutting and, again, the fact that I'm watching a movie. I know it's an odd thing to say, but that's always my goal—to forget it's a movie while I'm watching. I want to create a story in which the audience can be swept away completely and not land until it's over. That's always the objective. And it's a great North Star, because even to have a possibility of achieving this effect, everything—and I mean everything, every single element of the picture—has to be in alignment, deepening the story.

Bradley Cooper

INT. BEDROOM, THE DAKOTA - CONTINUOUS

We SEE AND HEAR the sounds of the Parade outside. Felicia sits upon the windowsill, smoking and waiting. A timid knock on the door.

LB (O.C.)
Darling?

FELICIA
Hmm.

We HEAR LB amble in and close the door behind him.

LB (O.C.)
For a second there I thought...
Well... It was quite a stunt that you pulled.

FELICIA
What?

LB (O.C.)
That was quite a stunt that you pulled.

FELICIA
What do you mean?

LB comes in, glasses still on. They hold both sides of the frame on opposite ends.

LB
Well, darling, you put the pillow outside with my slippers and toothpaste and a toothbrush, and I haven't seen you since. I understand you're angry with me --

LB moves toward the bar, but slams his shin against the coffee table on the way.

LB (CONT'D)
(the table)
Jesus Christ... But let's be reasonable.

He places the milk carton on the bar cart and takes off his Jacket.

FELICIA
There is a saying in Chile about never standing under a bird that's full of shit.

LB makes himself a drink.

FELICIA
And I have just been living under that fucking bird for so long it's actually become comedic.

LB
Well, I think...

(He sits down on the couch)

That you are letting your own sadness get the better of you...

FELICIA
-- Oh, just stop it! This has nothing to do with me...
No!... No!...

LB
Let me at least finish... Let me finish what I am going to say!

FELICIA
This has nothing to do with me. It's about you. So you should love it!

LB
Okay...

LB goes for the milk again.

FELICIA
You want to be sleepless and depressed and sick -- you want to be all those things so you can avoid fulfilling your obligations.

LB
What obligations?

FELICIA
To what you've been given, to the gift you've been given. My God!

LB
Oh please... Please. The gift comes with burdens, if you have any idea. I'm sorry to just admit it, but that's the truth.

FELICIA
Oh, the burden of feigning honesty and love?

FELICIA (CONT'D)
That, above all, you love people?

LB
That's right, I love people.

FELICIA
And it's from that wellspring of love that complications arise in your life?

LB
That's exactly right.

FELICIA
Oh, just wake up! Take off your glasses!

(He does)

Hate in your heart, and anger -- for so many things it's hard to count -- that's what drives you. Deep, deep anger drives you. You aren't up there on that podium allowing us all to experience the music the way it was intended. You are throwing it in our faces.

LB
How dare you.

FELICIA
How much we will never be able to... ever understand... and by us witnessing YOU do it so effortlessly, you hope we will know, really know, deep in our core, how less than we all are to you.

LB
How dare you... oh, please...

LB (CONT'D)
No, that's your issue, if

you're less than... Join the crowd, join the line of people that feel "less than" with me.

FELICIA
And it's your hubris that kills me. You prance around with all your dewy-eyed waiters Harry corrals for you, under the guise they have something intellectual to offer you, or that you are, dare I say, "teaching" them.

LB
At least my heart is open.

FELICIA
Oh my God... The audacity to say that. Have you forgotten about the four years when you couldn't decide whether you wanted to marry me?

LB
Maybe you only want the idea of me, the "idea." You have no need for the real thing. As Richard Chamberlain said in that dreadful film we saw last week, "*How could I ever compete with the man you think I am?*"

LB gets up toward the bar.

FELICIA
And thank God I met Dick so that I could fucking survive your indecision.

LB
Dick Hart. Richard fucking Hart. Yeah, who fucking died...

FELICIA
Yes, who loved me.

LB
Oh, and he's a corpse now, and I was the one who was a fool, waiting outside the fucking hospital like an idiot, in my truth.

Felicia finally stands, digs in.

FELICIA
Your "truth" is a fucking lie that sucks up all the energy in every room and gives the rest of us zero opportunity to live or even breathe as our "true" selves. Your "truth" makes you brave and strong and saps the rest of us of any kind of bravery or strength. Because it's so draining, Lenny, it's so fucking draining to love and accept someone who doesn't love and accept themselves. And that's the only truth I know about you.

They are now face-to-face.

FELICIA (CONT'D)
If you're not careful, you're going to die a lonely old queen.

ALEX (O.C.)
(calling out)
Mummy! Daddy!

NINA (O.C.)
(calling out)
Daddy! Look!

Knocking starts on the door...

NINA (O.C.)
(calling out)
Mummy! C'mon, you're going to
miss Snoopy!

ALEXANDER (O.S.)
(calling out)
Snoopy's here, hurry up!

We SEE a GIANT SNOOPY FLOAT pass the windows
as it moves down Park Avenue and in between LB
and Felicia.

NINA AND ALEXANDER (O.C.)
What are you guys doing in there?
You've been in there for ages. Dad!

LB
(calling back to them)
Yes...

FELICIA
I'll go.

And she leaves him alone as the family cheers
the parade and celebration below.

BEHIND THE CURTAIN

By Janet Maslin

When Mike Wallace interviewed Leonard Bernstein in 1979, he couldn't lay a glove on the maestro. Wallace was such a fan that Bernstein ran circles around him. Did Bernstein care about fame? Of course not! He was sixty, had been famous for thirty-five years and found it useful only for helping good causes. Money? Bernstein said he signed contracts without looking at them. Style? Bernstein zipped up his nearly open jacket, tousled his mane and asked if Wallace found that preferable. Game, set, match.

That was a performance. The real Bernstein was much more complicated, as Bradley Cooper's devastatingly nuanced *Maestro* makes clear. Here was an outsized public figure with the stature of a world leader and the private recklessness, too. Not for nothing were he and President John F. Kennedy near-contemporaries from eastern Massachusetts who personified sophistication and glamour. They were charismatic giants wielding global influence, and we aren't making any more of them.

Their wives shared common ground, too. Felicia Bernstein, born Felicia María Cohn Montealegre, had poise and elegance to rival that of First Lady Jacqueline Kennedy. She, too, also fell into a fairy-tale courtship that should have fulfilled her greatest expectations. As embodied with such dazzling archness by Carey Mulligan, young Felicia came to New York as an ambitious, talented actress and soon saw a soulmate in Bernstein. One of the many pleasures of *Maestro* is watching them meld together as they sit exchanging banter in a black-and-white pastoral setting. They forge a dream of romantic unity, but they sit back-to-back. That dream would become less attainable when they were figuratively face-to-face.

Not for nothing does an early *Maestro* poster depict the elegant Felicia with her back to the camera. If she wanted to partner with the rising star of the New York Philharmonic, her back would have to stay turned. She knew what a flirt Lenny was. She knew about his passionate affairs with men. She also knew it was worth a try and told him so. "I am willing to accept you as you are, without being a martyr or sacrificing myself on the L.B. altar," she wrote in a letter that outlined the way their prospective marriage might work. It was a good-faith offer. She thought it could happen. They both thought it could be grand.

What *Maestro* does so well is glide from this rapture to its unraveling. Cooper's use of lush black-and-white, as his film elides time and escapes daunting realities, has a breathless, dreamlike momentum. Lenny is always on the move, always bright-eyed with excitement, and Felicia keeps pace with him. Were his dalliances real? Were they playful or passionate? Could this be more than a marriage of convenience? The film bursts into full color just as Felicia's understanding does, and once again an old television clip is relevant. *Maestro* faithfully re-creates Edward R. Murrow's interview with the ravishing couple, but it reverses our point of view. In real time, audiences saw what Murrow did: the happy couple draped across a sofa, with both of them talking about Lenny's brilliant career. But Cooper starts out in a rear hallway, before the interview cameras roll. This, too, is a performance, and a not entirely successful one. They may have fooled Murrow, but they didn't fool each other.

It's revealing that Wallace's interview took place not long after Felicia's death in 1978. Bernstein was giddy with thoughts of new projects. If he'd suffered a great loss, it didn't show, although the film's framing device brings age and regret to the fore. *Maestro* is ultimately about how so much could become so little, about the way expectations can destroy hope, about the compromises we make and the disillusionment they can bring. To be sure, it's a film that hits the highest peaks of intoxicating joy. But its best moments explore the ease with which that joy can disappear. And in capturing the full arc of that turbulence, Cooper isn't just looking at one Camelot-caliber couple. He's turning a mirror on us all.

RE-CREATING FIVE TIME PERIODS

"I knew I wanted to shoot on film. And I knew for the first section I wanted to shoot in 35 millimeter black-and-white. The only way I felt that we could tell this story was to move from black-and-white to color and through multiple aspect ratios to convey the time periods from the '40s through the '80s."

BRADLEY COOPER

Maestro was primarily captured using two Panaflex Millennium XL cameras, with an additional Panaflex Millennium XL camera dedicated for Steadicam shots. Three primary Kodak film stocks were used: Eastman Double-X 5222, for our black-and-white scenes portraying L.B. and Felicia's early years; for scenes in color, Vision3 500T Color Negative Film 5219 was selected for interiors, and Vision3 200T Color Negative Film 5213 was used for exteriors. There were also specific instances where we employed the Vision3 250D Color Negative Film 5207, a medium-speed daylight-balanced film. The film was processed at FotoKem.

The film was shot in a 1.33:1 aspect ratio in its entirety, with the exception of the scenes which took place in 1989, for which we used a 1.85:1 aspect ratio.

Our lens choices leaned heavily on Panavision Vintage Prime lenses: The 29 mm T1.2 PVintage Ultra Speed lens was a favorite, followed closely by the 35 mm T1.6 PVintage Ultra Speed. Other frequently used lenses included the 24 mm T1.2 PVintage Ultra Speed, 50 mm T1.0 PVintage Ultra Speed and 21 mm T1.9 Primo. Occasionally, for specific visual requirements, we also employed the 75 mm T1.6 PVintage Ultra Speed, 100 mm T1.6 PVintage Ultra Speed and both the 40 mm T1.9 Primo Special Optics and the 40 mm T2 Normal Speed. The 27 mm T1.9 Primo and 65 mm T1.8 Primo Special Optics were used more sparingly, as were the 135 mm T2 Zeiss Super Speed (PV). There were also moments where we opted for Angénieux lenses, with variable focal lengths, such as 15-40 and 28-76, but these were rare.

We used various ND filters when needed, as well as polarizers and color-correction filters like the 85 series, orange-tinted filters primarily used to balance the color temperature of our film when shooting in daylight.

Our filming techniques included Steadicam, for much of the first half of the film; handheld, for the East Hampton sequences; crane and dolly shots throughout; stationary dolly; and more specialized approaches like remote head with jib setups, and spidercam systems, for instance when L.B. looks over Carnegie Hall, with the camera pushing him towards his debut performance.

For more dynamic shots, we had an array of cranes at our disposal, including the Scorpio 23' Technocrane, the Scorpio 30' Technocrane, the larger Moviebird 35'/45' crane and the Scorpio 45' Technocrane. These cranes were paired with a versatile range of heads: the Scorpio head, Libra head, Matrix head and ever-present Mo-Sys head, which we used throughout the production.

After filming, we ran the print through the digital-intermediate (DI) process with Stefan Sonnenfeld at Company3, whom I worked with extensively. Here, the 35 mm film was meticulously scanned into a digital format. This allowed for precise color grading, refining the film's look and feel and seamlessly integrating our visual effects. Every frame was optimized to ensure clarity and consistency. Sound was then synced, and the film was prepared for both 35 mm projection and digital formats.

Matty Libatique, *cinematographer*

1943

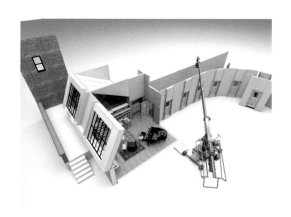

CARNEGIE
APARTMENT & HALLWAY

CARNEGIE HALL

"The opening at the Carnegie Hall apartment in the loft where he pulls the curtains open and then runs and he gets to Carnegie Hall down the hallway was so much fun. [Bradley] had this continuous shot in mind where we go from one location to another in the same shot, so we had to build the hallway of Carnegie Hall and then link it to the actual Carnegie Hall and the whole place. It had to be done in one shot with a big crane. It was an amazing camera move, and the wall fell away while we did it and had a huge track."

KEVIN THOMPSON, *production designer*

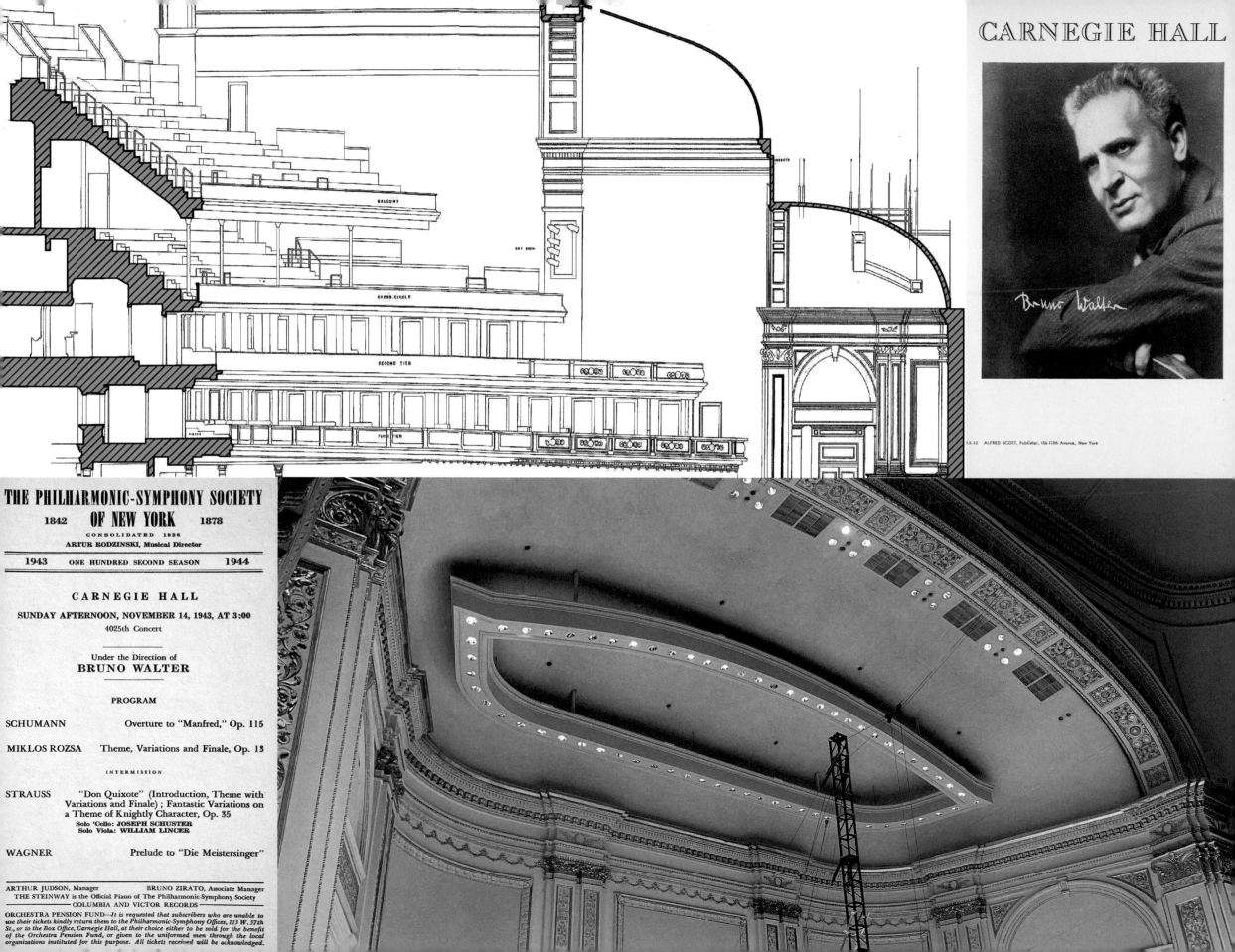

CARNEGIE HALL

BALCONY

DRESS CIRCLE

SECOND TIER

FIRST TIER

T-A-42   ALFRED SCOTT, Publisher, 156 Fifth Avenue, New York

Bruno Walter

THE PHILHARMONIC-SYMPHONY SOCIETY

1842   OF NEW YORK   1878

CONSOLIDATED 1928

ARTUR RODZINSKI, Musical Director

1943   ONE HUNDRED SECOND SEASON   1944

CARNEGIE HALL

SUNDAY AFTERNOON, NOVEMBER 14, 1943, AT 3:00

4025th Concert

Under the Direction of
BRUNO WALTER

PROGRAM

SCHUMANN	Overture to "Manfred," Op. 115
MIKLOS ROZSA	Theme, Variations and Finale, Op. 13

INTERMISSION

STRAUSS	"Don Quixote" (Introduction, Theme with Variations and Finale) ; Fantastic Variations on a Theme of Knightly Character, Op. 35
	Solo 'Cello: JOSEPH SCHUSTER Solo Viola: WILLIAM LINCER
WAGNER	Prelude to "Die Meistersinger"

ARTHUR JUDSON, Manager   BRUNO ZIRATO, Associate Manager
THE STEINWAY is the Official Piano of The Philharmonic-Symphony Society
COLUMBIA AND VICTOR RECORDS

ORCHESTRA PENSION FUND—It is requested that subscribers who are unable to use their tickets kindly return them to the Philharmonic-Symphony Offices, 113 W. 57th St., or to the Box Office, Carnegie Hall, at their choice either to be sold for the benefit of the Orchestra Pension Fund, or given to the uniformed men through the local organizations instituted for this purpose. All tickets received will be acknowledged.

1946

PROVINCETOWN PLAYHOUSE   BROADWAY HOUSE   ADELPHI THEATRE

"Working with the crew, and just communicating how important it was that the cinema of this feel like a memory, an imagination of these time periods, was so much fun. *A Star Is Born* was side to side. This movie is foreground-background because he's always heading towards something or being pulled from something."

BRADLEY COOPER

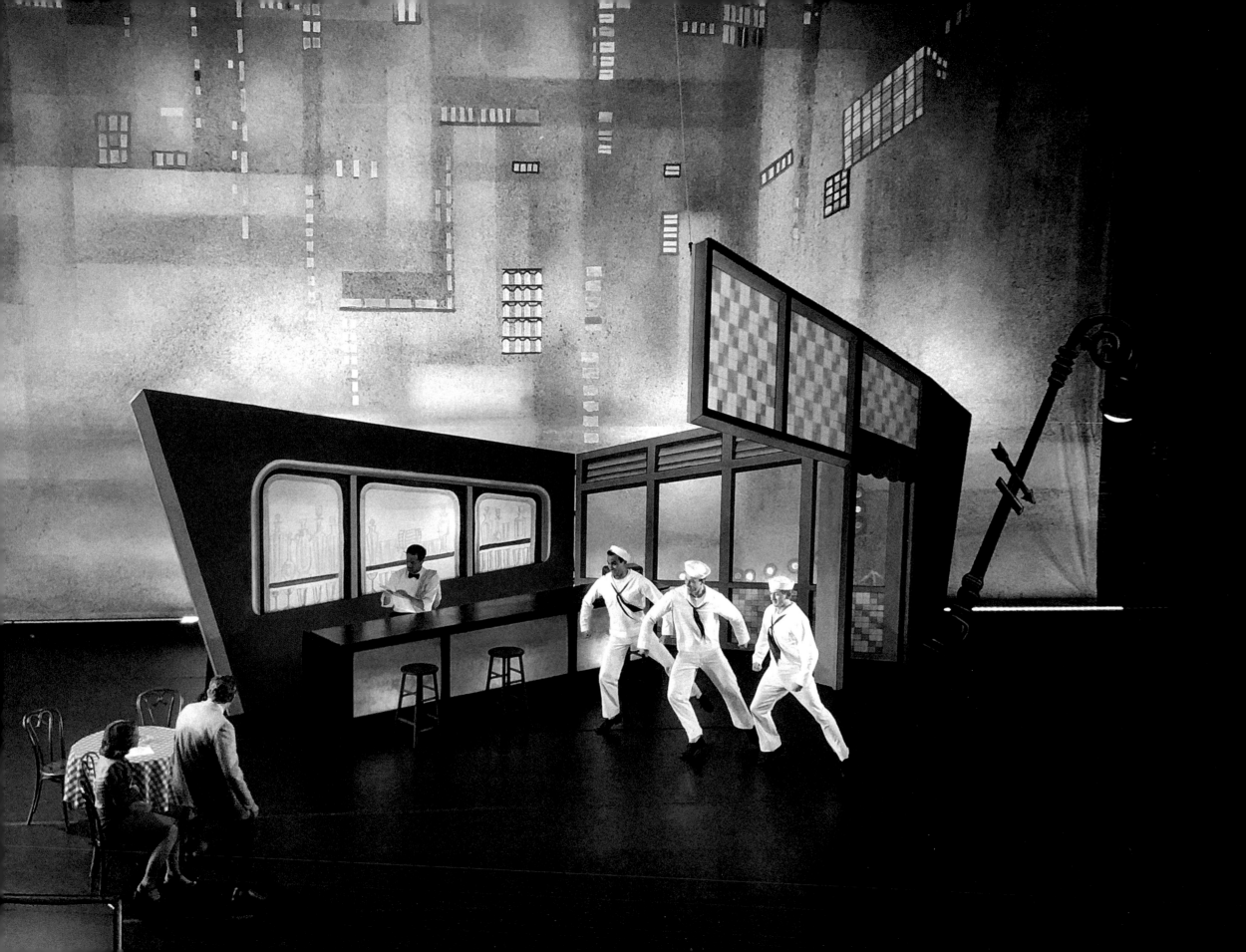

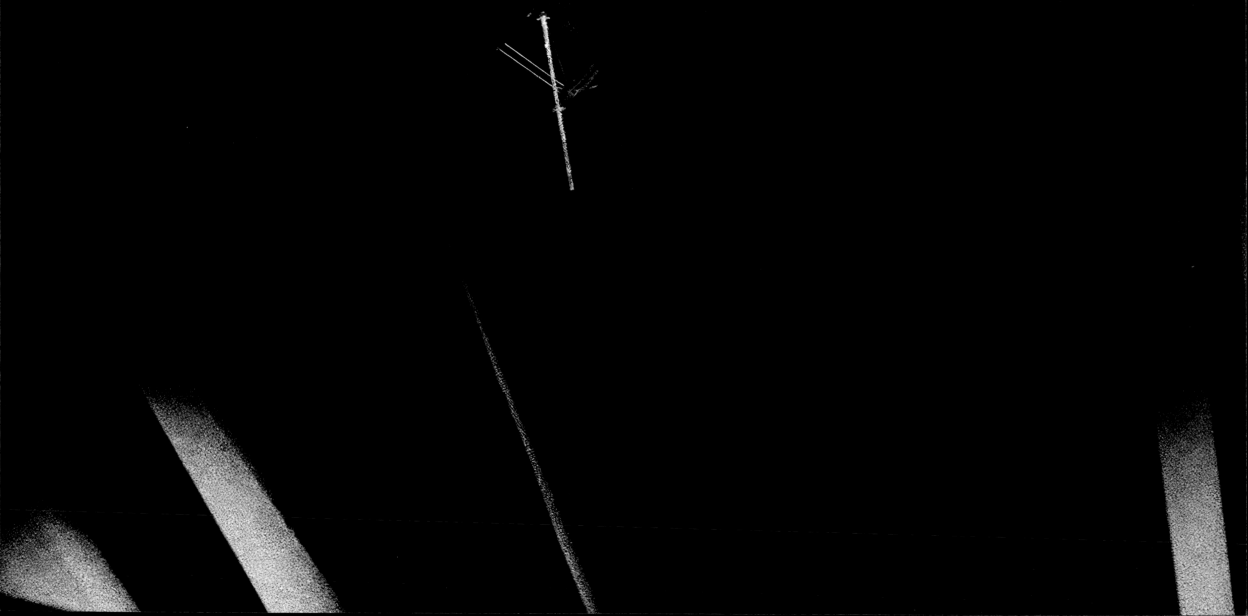

1955

OSBORNE APARTMENT

"Lenny lived a life of celebrity and creativity, and that's what Bradley lives. He's a storyteller, and there are many ways to tell a story—through music, through his acting, through writing, through directing. He does it all, just like Lenny."

MICHELLE TESORO, *editor*

1970 - 1971

FAIRFIELD HOUSE   THE DAKOTA   KENNEDY CENTER   WATERGATE HOTEL

"We actually had the chance to go to Fairfield and meet his daughter and get a tour. And we looked at some of his clothes that were still in the closet there, and we actually used one of his real robes. And Carey really wore one of Felicia's dresses. We didn't even have to tailor it—it just fit."

MARK BRIDGES, *costume designer*

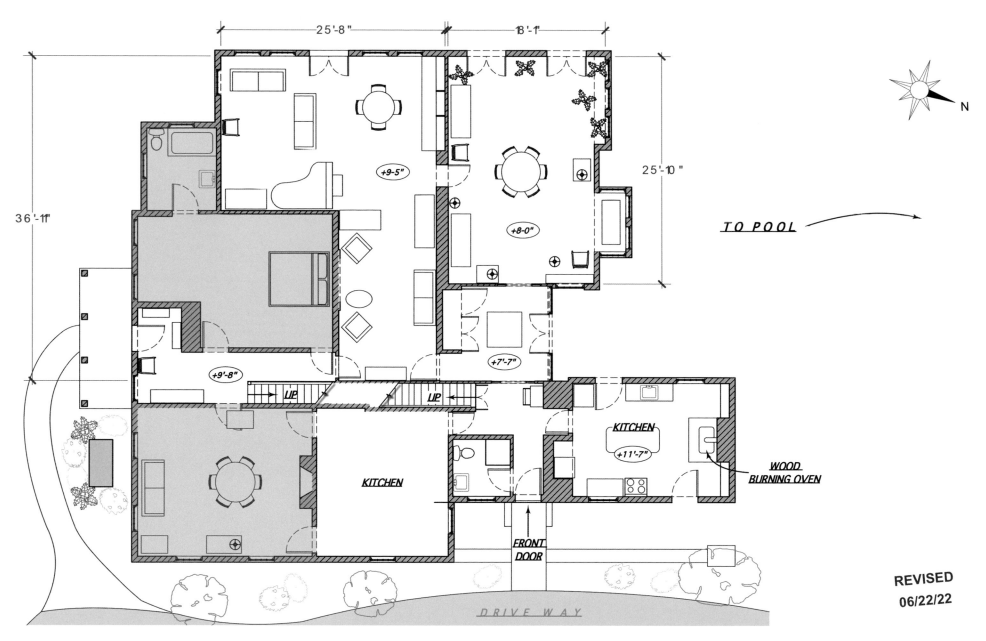

25'-8" 18'-1"

36'-11" 25'-10"

+9-5"

+8-0"

TO POOL

N

+9'-8"

+7'-7"

+11'-7"

UP UP

KITCHEN

KITCHEN

WOOD BURNING OVEN

FRONT DOOR

DRIVE WAY

REVISED
06/22/22

DIRECTOR'S PLAN - FIRST FLOOR

Scale: 1/8" = 1'-0"

0   10   20   30   40   50   60   70 FT

RYBERNIA

Director
BRADLEY COOPER

Production Designer
KEVIN THOMPSON

Supervising Art Direct
DEB JENSEN

SET NAME I/E - Fairfield House [First Floor]	SCALE 1/8" = 1'0"	SET NO. 124-
DRAWING Director's Plan	BY BAM	DATE 04/20/22	SHEET NO.
LOCATION 216 Dunham Road, Fairfield, CT 06824	SHOOTS	REVISED	DP

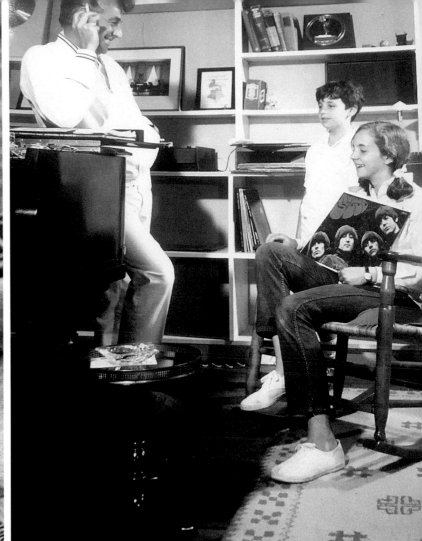

Leonard Bernstein with his daughter Jamie, circa 1950.

"In truth these people were fancy, but they were also not fancy. They were unpretentious. Their home in Fairfield and the beautiful Dakota apartment had things Felicia bought at flea markets, and she did a lot of decorating herself. The décor was sort of bohemian and helped set the mood for all of the interesting people that revolved around them."

KEVIN THOMPSON, *production designer*

"We re-created the Dakota apartment on a stage. They won't let you shoot in the Dakota, but Bradley and I went to the actual Bernstein apartment in the Dakota, and I could interpret it and sort of get the scale of things and duplicate the moldings and the sizes of the windows. So it is really close to what the actual apartment was."

KEVIN THOMPSON, *production designer*

The John F. Kennedy Center for the Performing Arts

PRESENTS

The World-Première Performance on
Wednesday Evening, September 8, 1971, at 7:30

of

LEONARD BERNSTEIN'S

MASS

A Theatre Piece For Singers, Players and Dancers

TEXTS FROM THE ROMAN LITURGY AND BY THE COMPOSER

Additional Texts by STEPHEN SCHWARTZ

Choreography by ALVIN AILEY

Settings by OLIVER SMITH Costumes by FRANK THOMPSON Lighting by GILBERT HEMSLEY, JR.

Musical Director MAURICE PERESS

with

THE NORMAN SCRIBNER CHOIR   THE BERKSHIRE BOYS' CHOIR

THE ALVIN AILEY AMERICAN DANCE THEATRE

Production Coordinator DIANA SHUMLIN

Directed by GORDON DAVIDSON

Produced by ROGER L. STEVENS   Associate Producer SCHUYLER G. CHAPIN

1973
-
1977

PALM COURT   ELY CATHEDRAL

1978

SUMMER HOUSE

"We were in Carnegie Hall, we went to Ely Cathedral in London, we went to Tanglewood, we visited their apartment in the Dakota to re-create it, we were in Central Park, we went to Fairfield, we shot in their home, in their bedroom, in their kitchen, in their pool. It was all real. It had to be."

BRADLEY COOPER

1989

TANGLEWOOD

"I want audiences to understand and appreciate who Leonard Bernstein was, and to also see his contributions to music, and how big of a star that he was. And also to understand the human heart doesn't always have a straight line."

MARK BRIDGES, *costume designer*

ANATOMY OF A SCENE

Fancy Free/On the Town

When tackling this type of journey in a film, I'm always looking to consolidate story and plot so that it won't be derivative for the audience. In *A Star Is Born,* I was able to forgo a montage of Ally's "rise to fame" by simply having her perform on *Saturday Night Live.* We get to see the transformation but also, in that one scene, how this ascension has affected both her and Jackson. "Ally sings as musical guest on *SNL*" is the plot point, and development of the relationship is the story.

There was a similar conundrum regarding the beginning of Lenny and Felicia's relationship. How can I best communicate how unique and complicated this was for both characters while also highlighting the joy of it all? To me, *Fancy Free* and *On the Town* were the perfect vessels. And I love that it's all revealed because of Felicia's agency—as it was in real life. She drags him away to this world of his music. There were many hurdles in pulling this whole idea off. Namely great dancers! Justin Peck and Craig Salstein were an invaluable part of this sequence. We spent weeks, months even, planning and choreographing. And we rehearsed on the set as well, thank goodness, before shooting. I knew I wanted a white sheet and black sailor ties, all floating around the frame, reminiscent of notes and sheet music. This was the guiding vision that helped link everything. This sequence helps articulate what Felicia is choosing to buy into. Lenny doesn't just want to fuck the sailor, he wants to be the sailor, and he wants her to love him as the sailor and to choose to be with him as the world tries to pull them apart. (Dick Hart, as a sailor, rushes to Felicia from backstage.) In the end, if they always come back to each other, they can survive and fend off all the hands.

I also wanted that triangular design of the sheet over the dancers to act as a transition to the bedsheets falling off their interlocked feet as we meet them postcoital on the bedroom floor. The shots and rhythm are all designed to build to that visual and story "climax." I even took a still frame of the feet under the sheet—as we had already shot that scene—and superimposed it over the frame, lining up the outline of the still with the shape of all the hands. It was a tedious undertaking, but I'm very grateful that the dancers were generous enough to allow me to move their fingers half an inch here or there. There were a lot of giggles.

Bradley Cooper

Editing this scene was pure joy. I love editing dance. I've edited ballet before, so in my mind I knew what we would be looking for from a dancer's perspective. You want to see the whole body. You also want to see the energy coming off of a finger without missing the emotion of the performance. The way Bradley directed it was quite tight—surgical.

In breaking down the scene in editorial, my assistants created one grouped clip of all the takes synced up to the music track. This made it easy to compare takes for different parts of the music. We had the scene from all sides, so we could choose the preferred performance.

The whole sequence is a true representation of their relationship—their life together and their obstacles to come. It beautifully conveys how they would always try to come together and then be pulled apart and then come together again. In this scene you feel that Felicia really sees Leonard very clearly. She sees who he is.

Michelle Tesoro, *editor*

FELICIA
Why would you ever want to give this
up? It's so wonderful.

LB
It's not serious music, is it?

FELICIA
What does that mean?

LB
It means... he thinks I could be
the first great American conductor.

FELICIA
Is that what you want?

LB
I want a lot of things...

We go into the kiss, close on them, their mouths together, the passion of their embrace as the top stage lights flair and BAM!!!

We hear the horn wail that marks the beginning of "On the Town" Act 1: Opening. This breaks their lips apart.

We PULL BACK and now the horns wail three more times. LB takes Felicia's hand and begins to pull her across the stage seemingly away from all this, but as they move, dancers pass us in the foreground and we see the entire set has transformed into the original production of "On the Town."

EXCITED SAILORS on leave dancing along with FEMALE CIVILIANS under what seems like a night sky filled with stars.

They are now enmeshed in one huge choreographed dance piece.

Within this, we realize one of the sailors staring at her is Dick Hart. He looks knowingly at her and she reacts... but she is pulled away as the tubas begin chortling through the familiar base line, dancers spinning around LB and Felicia bewildered.

Dancers begin running towards them from downstage, holding huge white sheets, the sheets billowing up and around them, enveloping the two of them and everyone else, including the frame until it backs away and is pulled off the stage, now revealing just Felicia and LB stranded alone.

And as the music crescendoes into the familiar open, we PUSH IN as LB and Felicia run and cling to each other, followed by all the dancers too, everyone coming together!!

THREE SAILORS (SINGING)
New York, New York!

ACKNOWLEDGMENTS

Kristie Macosko Krieger, Steven Spielberg, Martin Scorsese, Fred Berner, Amy During, Josh Singer, Mark Bridges, Kevin Thompson, Kazu Hiro, Michelle Tesoro, Sian Gregg, Kay Georgiou, Matthew Libatique, Yannick Nézet-Séguin, Jason MacDonald, Jamie Bernstein, Alexander Bernstein, Nina Bernstein, Heather Wallace, Janet Maslin, Rick Rubin, Lisa Taback, Chris Gonzalez, Erin Burbridge, Marla Weinstein, Katie Doyle, Catherine Rinaldo, Emily Frandsen, Sarah Rodman, Steven Newman, Trixie Textor, Charles Greene, Margaret Lewis, Monica Barraza-Wenham, Kelley Cribben and our Maestros: Leonard Bernstein and Felicia Cohn Montealegre Bernstein.

The publisher would like to thank the following: John Broderick; Kathleen Sabogal, Carnegie Hall Rose Archives; Brian Stehlin, Getty Images; David Grossman, Grossman Enterprises; Adam Stotlman, Ken Heyman; Hannah Middlebrook, The Kennedy Center Archives.

CREDITS

Unit photography by Jason MacDonald.
Film stills by Matthew Libatique.
Costume designs by Mark Bridges.
Costume illustrations by Phillip Boutté.
Production designs by Kevin Thompson.

Pp. 13, 163, 164, 168, 210 (bottom left): Alexios Chrysikos; pp. 26 (left): Photography courtesy of Library of Congress, Music Division (100030107); p. 31 (right): © John Broderick/Photography by Dan Weiner; pp. 36-37, 38-39, 40, 41, 42-43: Kazu Hiro; p. 66 (right): © Jack Mitchell/Getty Images; p. 69 (left): Photography courtesy of Library of Congress, Music Division (100030011); p. 77 (top left): Photography by Henry Grossman/© Grossman Enterprises, LLC. All Rights Reserved; p. 77 (top right): Courtesy of The Leonard Bernstein Office, Inc./Photography courtesy of Library of Congress, Music Division (100030100); pp. 77 (bottom left), 77 (bottom right): © Ken Heyman; pp. 154, 169 (bottom right): Jurasama Arunchai; pp. 169 (top left), 208, 240-241: Brett Martinez; pp. 169 (top right), 169 (bottom left): Courtesy of Carnegie Hall Rose Archives; pp. 170, 188, 193, 194, 198-199, 203 (second from left), 203 (right), 210 (bottom right), 212, 216 (top), 217, 226 (right), 228, 231, 232, 236, 237, 242, 249, 253, 260-261: Kevin Thompson; pp. 175 (left), 175 (middle), 176, 180, 190-191, 210 (top left), 210 (top middle), 264, 265: Samson Jacobson; p. 209: Ryan Heck; p. 210 (top right): Courtesy of The Leonard Bernstein Office, Inc.; p. 211 (right): © Bettmann/Getty Images; pp. 214, 215: Deborah Jensen; p. 226 (left): Courtesy of the Kennedy Center Archives.

Every possible effort has been made to identify and contact all rights holders and obtain their permission for work appearing in these pages. Any errors or omissions brought to the publisher's attention will be corrected in future editions.

Slipcase: © Assouline.
Hardcover (front and back): Matthew Libatique.
Endpages: Matthew Libatique.

All Leonard Bernstein quotes © Amberson Holdings LLC,
used by permission of the Leonard Bernstein Office Inc.

Creative director: Jihyun Kim
Senior editor: Scout Sabo
Designer: Dylan Brackett
Senior photo editor: Andrea Ramírez Reyes
Photo editor: Ginger Ooi

© Netflix 2023
© 2023 Assouline Publishing
3 Park Avenue, 27th floor
New York, NY 10016 USA
Tel: 212-989-6769   Fax: 212-647-0005
assouline.com

Printed in Italy by Grafiche Milani.
ISBN: 9781649803177